WILD

ANIMALS

Lynn Huggins-Cooper

QEB

Quarto is the authority on a wide range of topics.

Quarto educates, entertains and enriches the lives of
our readers—enthusiasts and lovers of hands-on living.

www.quartoknows.com

Author: Lynn Huggins-Cooper
Editorial: Carly Madden and Victoria Garrard
Design: Jacqueline Palmer
Cover design: Mike Henson

© 2020 Quarto Publishing plc

First published in 2020 by QEB Publishing,
an imprint of The Quarto Group.
26391 Crown Valley Parkway, Suite 220
Mission Viejo, CA 92691, USA
T: +1 949 380 7510
F: +1 949 380 7575
www.QuartoKnows.com

A CIP record for this book is available from
the Library of Congress.

ISBN 978-0-7112-5359-9

Manufactured in Guangdong, China TT102019
9 8 7 6 5 4 3 2 1

Contents

Watch out!

From tropical **rain forests** to dry deserts, from parks to our own homes, creepy crawlers are everywhere—so watch out!

△ *Weta are large wingless crickets from New Zealand.*

Different types

A lot of the creepy crawlers we see around us are insects. All insects, such as beetles, wasps, and ants, have six legs and three body parts. There are over a million different **species** of insects. Other creepy crawlers include spiders and, in the oceans, **crustaceans** such as crabs and shrimps.

Creepy?

Although many people are scared of insects and other creepy crawlers, they really are amazing creatures. They can survive in the most hostile environments, including places that people cannot live.

◁ *Scientists believe that over 90 percent of all the creatures alive today are insects.*

Large ancestors

Some creepy crawlers are huge. The Malaysian giant stick insect, for example, grows about as long as a man's arm. But today's creepy crawlers are small compared to creatures from **prehistoric** times. Some 390 million years ago, 8-feet long (2.4-meter) sea scorpions swam in the oceans and 10-feet long (3-meter) centipedes scurried through the forests.

▷ Goliath beetles are thought to be the largest, heaviest insects in the world.

Cool fish

Freaky fish are found everywhere, from the depths of the oceans to muddy riverbeds. At least 28,000 species of fish are known to exist.

△ **Aquarium** fish are bred in captivity rather than being caught in the wild.

Fun fact!

The great white shark has 300 sharp, triangular teeth.

△ The great white shark has a terrible reputation for being a **maneater**, and has been over-hunted because of this.

Endangered

The International Union for Conservation of Nature states that 1,414 species of fish are threatened with **extinction**. Fish are at risk because too many are taken from the oceans by fishermen and their habitats are being destroyed by pollution.

△ *The whale shark is the world's largest species of fish. It can be up to 50 feet long (14 meters).*

Save our fish

There is a huge variety of life in our lakes, rivers, seas, and oceans. Some fish are cleverly **camouflaged**, some are extremely poisonous, and there is even a vicious vampire fish that sucks the blood of other fish. All fish are worth protecting.

Freaky flyers

The world is full of amazing birds. They come in all shapes and sizes, from tiny wrens and hummingbirds to huge birds of prey. Bats and insects fly too...

▽ Most species of hummingbird can hover in midair. They do this by flapping their wings about 50 times per second.

△ Many birds carry food to their young in their stomach.

All shapes of beaks

Some birds have developed special features for survival. Hummingbirds have long, pointed beaks that they poke deep into flowers so they can drink the **nectar**.

Horrid habits

Birds have many habits that we might think of as unpleasant. These include feeding their young with **regurgitated** food. Fruit bats, or flying foxes, like sweet, juicy fruit, just like we do!

Fun fact!

The vampire bat drinks the blood of living creatures.

△ *After feeding on fruit, the fruit bat licks its claws clean.*

Cold blood

Both **amphibians** and reptiles are cold-blooded animals, which means that their body temperature is the same as the temperature of the surrounding air.

△ Like modern crocodiles, the **dinosaur T-rex** had sharp teeth for grabbing food.

▽ *Many salamanders do not have lungs or* **gills**. *They get the oxygen they need through their skin.*

Reptiles old and new

Dinosaurs were reptiles that lived millions of years ago. Like modern reptiles, they had no fur and they hatched from eggs. Dinosaurs are now **extinct**.

Amphibians

Amphibians have **adapted** to life in and out of water. They are able to breathe through their skin, although most adult amphibians also have lungs for breathing. Some amphibians produce **toxins** in their skin that make them taste bad to predators.

▽ *Poison dart frogs have poisonous skin.*

Fun fact!

Local tribes people in South America rub poison dart frogs against the skin of young parrots so they grow different colored feathers!

Really wild!

The animal world is full of amazing creatures. The sweetest-looking animals may be very fierce, and creatures that look scary may actually be gentle and shy.

△ Weasels are fierce predators. They have beautiful fur like a cat, but you cannot stroke them!

Bad behavior?

Animals kill other animals because they need to eat. All wild animals can be dangerous. If a man enters a bear's territory, the bear may follow its instincts and attack, just as it would if any other wild animal threatened its territory. Its behavior is natural wild animal behavior.

◁ Bears will attack if they are surprised, or are protecting their territory or **cubs**.

▷ Leafy sea dragons are a type of fish. Their leafy **appendages** may look strange, but they help sea dragons to hide among floating seaweed.

Fun fact!

The leafy sea dragon uses its long snout to suck up food.

Terrors of the deep

Some fish have terrifying teeth, others have small, light-producing cells on their bodies, which attract **prey**.

△ *At night, marine hatchetfish rise to a depth of 164 feet (50 meters) below the surface to feed.*

Marine hatchetfish

Marine hatchetfish live at depths of 650 to 19,680 feet (200 to 6,000 meters). Small cells, called **photophores**, on the undersides of their bodies give off tiny spots of light that point downward.

Spookfish

Spookfish, also known as barreleyes, live at depths of 1,310 to 8,200 feet (400 to 2,500 meters). Their sensitive eyes point upward and are able to detect **predators** swimming in the dim water above them.

◁ *The bones of a barreleye's skull are so thin that you can see its brain between its eyes.*

▷ *The barbeled dragonfish is a fierce predator in spite of its small size.*

Barbeled dragonfish

Barbeled dragonfish live in oceans at depths of up to 4,920 feet (1,500 meters). The female has a long growth under its lower jaw that produces light at the tip.

Fun fact!

The young of some dragonfish have eyes on the end of long stalks, unlike their parents.

15

Funky frogs

Frogs live all over the world, except in icy **Antarctica**. Most species live in **tropical** countries with warm, damp climates, but some prefer hot deserts.

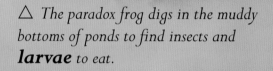

△ *The paradox frog digs in the muddy bottoms of ponds to find insects and* **larvae** *to eat.*

Paradox frog

The paradox frog lives in ponds and lakes in South America and on the Caribbean island of Trinidad. Adult paradox frogs are smaller than their **tadpoles**. As the tadpoles develop into adults, they shrink.

▽ *At only 1 inch (2.5 cm) long, the pouched frog is about the size of a cherry.*

Pouched frog

The female pouched frog lays a pile of eggs in damp soil rather than in water. As the eggs hatch, the male hops into the middle of the pile, and the tadpoles wriggle into two pouches above his back legs. The tadpoles stay in his pouches until they are fully formed frogs.

Fun fact!

In 2016, 10,000 Lake Titicaca frogs died due to pollution in the Coata River.

Lake Titicaca frog

The Lake Titicaca frog lives only in Lake Titicaca in South America. The lake is 12,500 feet above sea level so the air is very thin. To cope with these conditions, the frog has developed saggy skin with many folds. The frog soaks up lots of oxygen through its extra skin.

▽ *The Lake Titicaca frog can survive underwater as it absorbs oxygen from the water through its skin.*

Foul feeders

Some birds, such as vultures, eat **carrion**. Turkey vultures sometimes regurgitate what they have eaten because the smell of rotting food puts off predators.

△ *The hoatzin cannot fly well making it vulnerable to predators, such as monkeys.*

Hoatzin

The hoatzin is a South American cuckoo that smells of cow manure! It uses **bacteria** to **ferment** plant materials in the front part of its gut. This helps the bird to digest its food. The strong smell puts off predators.

Gannets

Gannets are seabirds. They often regurgitate the contents of their stomach if they are disturbed or alarmed.

◁ *A baby gannet will tap its mother's beak to get her to regurgitate a meal of partially digested fish.*

Vultures

Vultures are **scavengers**—they eat the remains of dead animals that have been killed by predators, such as lions. Vultures have amazingly strong acid in their stomach to help them digest food. Some vultures can even digest bones.

Most vultures have a bald head. Feathers would be difficult to keep clean as the birds feed on carcasses.

▽ *Different species of vulture feed on the same carcass at different times. White-backed vultures (shown here) eat the insides of the carcass.*

Spooky spiders

Some spiders leap out
and ambush their victims.
Others inject poison
when they bite.

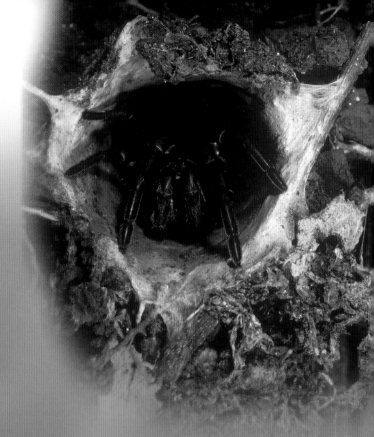

△ A funnel web spider sits at the entrance to its burrow, ready to pounce.

Tarantulas

There are an incredible 800 to
1,000 species of tarantulas living
in warm parts of the world.
They eat insects, other spiders,
small **reptiles**, frogs, and even
small birds.

Funnel web spiders

Funnel web spiders live in Australia.
They have sharp, strong **fangs** that
they use to inject **venom** into their
prey. Their venomous bites can
cause serious illness or death
in humans.

◁ Although venomous,
no one is known to
have died as a result
of a tarantula bite.

▽ *The female golden orb web spider strings her webs between trees.*

Golden orb web spiders

Golden orb web spiders live in Africa and Australia. The spiders are small, but their webs can be up to 6.5 feet (2 meters) wide, and can last for several years. The silk is so strong that it has been used in the South Pacific to make fishing nets.

Fun fact!

"Golden" in the golden orb web spider's name describes the color of the web, rather than the spider itself.

Clever tricks

Some fish perform amazing tricks to keep themselves safe and to catch prey.

△ *The royal gramma lives among the coral reefs of the Caribbean Sea.*

Porcupine pufferfish

The porcupine pufferfish eats small creatures and shellfish that it finds on the ocean floor. Feelers hanging down from its nostrils help it to find food.

Royal gramma

The royal gramma is half purple and half yellow. Its attractive colors make it a popular aquarium fish. All the young are born as females but the females can change to become males if there are not enough males about. Amazing!

◁ *When the porcupine pufferfish is alarmed, it **inflates** itself by swallowing water.*

▷ *The male Siamese fighting fish looks after his bubble nest.*

Siamese fighting fish

Siamese fighting fish are found in **rice paddies**, ponds, and streams in Asia. As the female lays her eggs, the male fish catches them in his mouth and spits them into a nest of bubbles that he has made.

Fun fact!

A male Siamese fighting fish is aggressive toward other males, and will even attack its own reflection in a mirror!

23

Slimy snails

Snails are found all over the world. Their shells give them protection from predators and the drying effects of the wind and sun.

Periwinkles

Periwinkles are snails that live on the seashore. To stop itself from drying out at low tide, a periwinkle uses slime to seal the gap between its shell and the plant or rock it is on.

△ *Periwinkles are a favorite food of many seabirds.*

Giant African land snails

There are three species of giant African land snail. They are found in many warm, tropical countries. One species, the East African land snail eats rotting plants, fruit, and vegetables, as well as bones and shells that provide **calcium** to make its own shell strong.

◁ *A baboon inspects a giant African land snail.*

Fun fact!

Garden snails are so good at digesting that they even eat damp paper and cardboard.

Brown garden snail

The brown garden snail is common in the UK and Europe. It feeds on rotting plants, **algae, fungi**, and **lichen**. It is most active in wet weather and at night. If the weather gets too dry, the snail goes into its shell and seals the entrance.

▷ *The brown garden snail has a long tongue, called a* **radula***, covered in horny teeth.*

25

Beastly biters

Alligators, crocodiles, and the Indian gharial have lots of terrifying teeth!

Alligators

There are two species of alligator—the huge American alligator and the much smaller Chinese alligator, which is almost extinct. Alligators live in swamps, freshwater ponds, rivers, and **wetlands**.

△ *The male gharial has a small growth on the end of its snout. It uses this to make a humming noise that warns off other males.*

Indian gharial

The Indian gharial lives in small numbers in the rivers of northeast India, Bangladesh, Nepal, and Bhutan. Large males can reach almost 20 feet long (6 meters). The Indian gharial catches small fish and other creatures by snapping its jaws as it sweeps its head from side to side.

▽ *An alligator kills its prey, such as this brown pelican, by gripping it and pulling it underwater until it drowns.*

Caimans

Caimans are the largest predators in South America's **Amazon basin**. They can reach up to 16 feet (5 meters) long—the length of an average station wagon. Caimans eat fish, turtles, birds, deer, **tapirs**, and even **anacondas**.

Fun fact!

Caimans crowding together in small ponds have been known to eat each other.

▽ *An adult caiman swallows a large fish whole. The acid in the caiman's stomach is so strong that it can digest every part of its prey!*

27

Putrid parasites

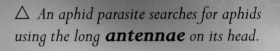

Parasites are creatures that live by feeding off another living creature, called the host.

△ *An aphid parasite searches for aphids using the long* **antennae** *on its head.*

▽ *The* **eyestalks** *of this snail are infected with parasitic flatworms.*

Aphid parasites

Aphid parasites are tiny black wasps. An adult lays its egg inside an aphid. The egg hatches and the parasite develops into an adult wasp. The wasp leaves its host by cutting a circular hole in the aphid and flying out.

Parasitic flatworms

One species of parasitic flatworm preys on birds. It starts life as an egg, found in a bird's droppings. A snail eats the bird's droppings and the flatworm's egg hatches inside the snail. The flatworm moves through the snail, and settles in one of its eyestalks. A bird eats the snail, and the flatworm ends up inside the bird's stomach, where it lays its eggs. The cycle then begins again…

Ichneumon wasps

There are thousands of species of ichneumon wasps. Females have a long tube, called an ovipositor, at the end of their body, which they use to inject their eggs into other animals.

◁ *Some species of ichneumon wasps lay their eggs under tree bark, in tunnels made by wood wasp larvae.*

Dirty defenses

Birds have developed many different ways to defend themselves from predators, some of which are quite unpleasant!

△ *The northern shoveler has a long, spoon-shaped bill for feeding from the water.*

Northern shoveler

The northern shoveler is a **dabbling duck**. If disturbed by a predator, the female shoveler sprays foul-smelling **feces** over her eggs to discourage the predator from eating them.

Fun fact!

The giant petrel is also known as a "stinker" due to the foul-smelling oil that it vomits at predators!

Petrels

A petrel's stomach contains a thick, strong-smelling oil that they vomit at intruders. The oil makes feathers less waterproof, so it is dangerous for other birds.

◁ *The petrel makes its nest in pebble-lined rock crevices.*

Fulmars

If an intruder approaches a fulmar's nest, the fulmar makes a coughing noise and then spits oil at the attacker. Even fulmar chicks can do this. Very young chicks can spit small amounts of oil as soon as they leave the egg. By the time they are four days old, they can fire oil a distance of 12 inches (30 centimeters)!

▽ *The fulmar lays its egg on a grassy cliff edge. Once the chick is about two weeks old, the adult birds leave the nest to search for food.*

△ *Fulmar chicks use their spitting skills to defend themselves against feral cats, otters, skuas, crows, and gulls.*

Peculiar predators

Some fish eat fish bigger than themselves. Others slash at their prey with a sword!

▽ *Oarfish have no teeth. They sieve small creatures through* **gill rakers** *in their mouths.*

Swordfish

The swordfish is named after its long, sharp bill, which looks like a sword. The fish can grow up to 15 feet long (4.5 meters). Feeding mostly at night, it uses its snout to slash at prey. The swordfish rises to the surface looking for fish, such as mackerel, as well as squid.

Oarfish

There are four species of oarfish, or ribbonfish, one of which is the longest **bony fish** in the sea. It can grow to an incredible 50 feet long (15.5 meters)—about the width of a basketball court. Oarfish live in the deep ocean and have rarely been seen alive.

Black swallower

The black swallower is a light-producing fish. It has the amazing ability to stretch its stomach up to three times its size when it eats, so that it can eat fish bigger than itself.

△ *The black swallower opens its mouth wide to eat fish whole and then slowly digests the food.*

◁ *The swordfish uses its bill to defend itself from predators, such as the shortfin mako shark.*

Fun fact!

Swordfish have been known to push their swords through the sides of small fishing boats.

33

Weird and wonderful

Some fish look as though they have come straight from the pages of a comic. One even has a mouth like a cartoon duck!

Fun fact!

The name "snipe eel" comes from the jaws of the fish, which look like the bill of a wading bird called a snipe.

Tripod fish

The tripod fish stands on its three long fins and waits for tiny crustaceans to bump into the fins near its head. Then the fish grasps its prey with these fins and directs the prey into its mouth.

◁ The tripod fish only grows up to 14.5 inches long (37 centimeters), but its three long fins may extend to nearly 3 feet long (one meter)!

Snipe eels

Snipe eels can be as long as 5 feet (1.5 meters). Their two jaws bend away from each other at the tips, and their teeth hook backward. This helps them to catch shrimps. Snipe eels prefer to swim in open water.

△ *Snipe eels swim with their mouths open, and catch the long antennae of passing shrimps on the hooked teeth on their jaws.*

Shovelnose guitarfish

The shovelnose guitarfish was living before the time of dinosaurs. It lives in the **Gulf of California**, and is shaped roughly like a guitar. It has lots of small, round teeth that look a little like rocks.

▷ *The shovelnose guitarfish prefers to live in shallow water. Buried in the sandy seabed, it can be difficult to spot.*

Nasty noses

Some animals have amazing noses, which they use to seek out food.

△ *The star-nosed mole's tentacles help it to identify prey by touch, as it is blind.*

Star-nosed mole

The star-nosed mole of North America looks like an ordinary mole—except for its nose. 22 fleshy tentacles stick out from the nose and help the mole to feel movements in the ground made by its prey.

Aardvark

The aardvark lives in Africa in the area south of the Sahara Desert. It has a long **snout**, which it uses to sniff out its food—ants and termites—as it walks along at night. It also listens for any sound of movement made by the termites.

▷ *When an aardvark digs a burrow or breaks into a termite mound, it can squeeze its nostrils shut to keep out the dust.*

▷ *The nose of the male proboscis monkey can be up to 5.5 inches long (14 centimeters).*

Fun fact!

A male proboscis monkey pushes its nose out of the way when it eats!

Proboscis monkey

The proboscis monkey is named after the large, wobbly nose, or "proboscis," of the male monkey. It is thought that the large nose helps the male to attract a mate. It lives in the swampy mangrove forests of Borneo.

Poisonous pests

Some reptiles and amphibians are very poisonous. They might have poison in their skin, their **saliva**, or their venomous fangs.

▽ The horned viper has two long scales on its head that look like horns.

Horned viper

When hunting, the horned viper digs its body into the sand and lies in wait. The only parts of the snake that remain visible are its horns. When prey approaches it strikes, shooting poison from its fangs. The horned viper preys on unwary **rodents**, such as rats, as well as small snakes and birds.

△ *The Gila monster has powerful claws for digging burrows but kills with poisonous saliva.*

Gila monster

The Gila monster is a lizard. It kills and eats birds, rodents, and other lizards by biting them and then chewing until venomous saliva flows into the wound. Its teeth are loose and if a few get broken, it just grows some more.

Poison dart frogs

Poison dart frogs are found in Central and South America and most are brightly colored. They **secrete**, or release, poison through their skin.

▷ *The most toxic poison dart frog is the golden poison frog, which carries enough poison to kill up to ten humans.*

Scavengers

Lots of birds find their food by scavenging. They may eat parts of carcasses left behind by other animals, or they may scavenge for food in garbage bins.

△ *The carrion crow's beak is thick and has a curved tip, ideal for picking up and carrying eggs.*

Carrion crow

The carrion crow is a large, black bird that likes to sit on the top of isolated trees. It watches birds building their nests, and later attacks them, eating their eggs and young.

Crested caracara

The crested caracara, or Mexican eagle, is the national bird of Mexico. It prefers to eat carrion in the form of dead and rotting fish, or roadkill.

◁ *The male caracara often acts as a lookout, watching for danger from a perch near its nest, to protect its young.*

Marabou stork

The marabou stork is a large bird. Its wingspan can reach a huge 10.5 feet (3.2 meters). The marabou stork scavenges on carrion and scraps. This may sound unpleasant, but it helps prevent the spread of diseases.

Fun fact!

Marabou storks march in front of grass fires, snatching and eating the small animals that are fleeing.

▷ *The marabou stork's featherless head and neck are easy to keep clean as it feeds.*

Sneaky salamanders

If a predator grabs the salamander by the tail, part of the tail breaks off and wriggles around. This distracts the predator so the salamander can run away unharmed.

Fire salamander

The fire salamander lives in the forests of southern and central Europe. It hunts during the night for insects, spiders and other small creatures. When it is not hunting, it hides under stones and logs.

Mole salamanders

Mole salamanders live in North America, in woodland and grassland areas. They live in burrows that they have dug, or in holes that have been abandoned by other small creatures.

◁ *Mole salamanders have smooth, shiny skin that can absorb oxygen.*

▽ If threatened, the
fire salamander sprays
a poisonous, milky fluid
from glands along its
back at the predator.

Hellbenders

Hellbenders, or giant
salamanders, live in Japan,
China, and North America.
Hellbenders eat virtually
any living thing that they
find in the water,
including **crayfish**,
worms, and insects.

Fun fact!

In North America,
hellbenders have
many names
including devil dog
and snot otter!

▷ *Hellbenders
have wrinkly skin
that oozes slime.*

Loathsome legs

Spiders are not the only animals with scary legs. The massive Japanese spider crab has ten of them!

Japanese spider crab

The Japanese spider crab lives in the Pacific Ocean around Japan. Using its two front legs, which are specialized for feeding, it eats mainly dead animals and shellfish that it finds on the seabed.

△ *Scolopendra centipedes grasp their prey with the claws on the ends of their powerful legs.*

Scolopendra centipedes

Scolopendra centipedes can be more than 12 inches long (30 centimeters). Most scolopendra centipedes are **nocturnal**. Using a pair of poison claws directly under the head, they bite their prey again and again, injecting it with venom.

◁ *The Japanese spider crab has a legspan about as long as a small car.*

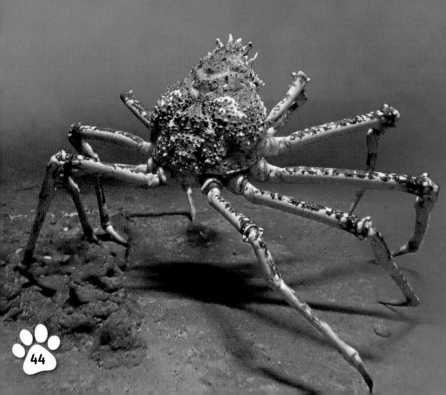

▽ *The basic structure of a harvestman has not changed much in 400 million years.*

Harvestmen

Harvestmen belong to a big family—there are more than 6,400 species worldwide. They eat flies, mites, small slugs, spiders, decaying plants, fungi, and bird droppings. After each meal, the harvestman pulls each of its eight legs through its jaws, one at a time, to clean them.

Fun fact!

If a harvestman is attacked and loses a leg, the leg continues to twitch. The predator is distracted and the harvestman escapes.

Poisonous animals

Some animals use venom for defense. Others use it to catch larger prey.

△ *The duck-billed platypus has a flat bill like a duck's beak*

Duck-billed platypus

The duck-billed platypus lives in eastern Australia. The male platypus has a **spur** on each of its back legs, which holds a strong poison. The poison is strong enough to kill a dog.

Solenodons

The two species of solenodon are both **endangered**. When a solenodon attacks its prey, such as a spider, poisonous saliva flows out of its lower front teeth. The poison stuns the prey, making it easier to grasp.

◁ *Solenodons run on their toes, and often trip over if they try to run too fast.*

▽ *Here, a diamondback rattlesnake is having its venom removed. The venom is used to make antivenom, a medicine used to treat snake bites.*

Pit vipers

Pit vipers are venomous snakes. They can sense body heat, which enables them to sneak up on their prey at night. Their hollow fangs inject poison into their prey.

Fun fact!

Many pit vipers are hunted and killed for their skins, which are used to make shoes and belts.

Vicious animals

Animals, such as killer whales, tigers, and bears, are well known for being fierce, but small creatures can also hunt aggressively.

△ Both northern and southern (above) short-tailed shrews use a special **toxin** to paralyze larger prey.

Northern short-tailed shrew

The northern short-tailed shrew needs to eat three times its body weight each day, so it spends its time hunting for insects, spiders, worms, and snails.

▽ *Weasels prey on mice, voles, frogs, birds, and rabbits. They eat eggs, too!*

Weasels

Weasels live mainly in the **northern hemisphere**. The weasel is a savage hunter. When excited, weasels do a strange, hopping war dance. Some **biologists** believe they perform the dance to confuse their prey.

Tasmanian devil

The Tasmanian devil looks like a small bear and is very vicious. It uses its powerful jaws to crack bones and tear fur and flesh. As well as feeding on carrion, it also eats the larvae of some types of beetle.

▽ *The Tasmanian devil was named "devil" because of the high-pitched screeching noises it makes at night.*

Fun fact!

When disturbed, Tasmanian devils can produce a stinky odor to rival that of a skunk.

49

Slimy pond life

Hiding behind rocks and slithering through weeds, ponds are full of slimy creatures of all shapes and sizes.

△ *A medicinal leech has three jaws that move backward and forward as the leech drinks blood.*

Medicinal leech

The medicinal leech uses **suction** and slime to attach itself to its prey, or to a person. As it sucks the blood of its prey, the leech dribbles saliva into the wound, making the blood easier to drink.

Fun fact! *The body of a medicinal leech stretches to about 10 times its original size as it fills with blood.*

Newts

Newts spend part of their time on land, but they start their lives in fresh water. Newts lay a single egg on plants in ponds or slow-moving streams. The egg hatches into a larva with feathery gills. Gradually the gills get smaller and the larva grows legs. The young newt, called an eft, is then able to leave the water.

▽ *The poisonous slime of the rough-skinned newt will kill most predators except the common gartersnake, which is* **immune** *to the poison.*

△ *Sludge worms live with their heads stuck in the mud and their tails waving in the water.*

Sludge worm

The sludge worm lives in large colonies on the bottom of ponds. It can survive even in very polluted water.

Beware dragons!

Some reptiles look like dragons and are even called dragons!

△ *The Chinese water dragon can sense light through a small bump on the top of its head called a "**third eye**."*

Komodo dragon

The Komodo dragon of Indonesia is the largest species of lizard. It has a big appetite and can eat up to 80 percent of its body weight in one meal.

Chinese water dragon

The Chinese water dragon lives in the rain forests of Southeast Asia. It often sits on branches overhanging water and can stay underwater for up to 30 minutes. The Chinese water dragon eats insects, small fish, rodents, and plants.

▽ *The Komodo dragon's saliva is filled with bacteria that help to kill its prey quickly.*

Fun fact!

Green iguanas' tails can break off when grabbed, but they will grow back!

Green iguana

The green iguana looks like a wingless dragon. Although it looks fierce, it is an herbivore, which means it eats only plants. It lives in Central and South America.

△ *The green iguana's long fingers and claws enable it to climb trees and cling onto branches.*

Bizarre birds

From birds with strange beaks to birds with peculiar habits, there are some very bizarre birds in the world.

▷ *The spoonbill's beak has lots of detectors inside that feel vibrations.*

Secretary bird

The secretary bird has an unusual habit—it stamps hard on grassy **tussocks** with its feet. This scares any small lizards, **mammals**, birds, or grasshoppers that may be hiding there. As they run away, the secretary bird stamps on them to stun or squash them.

◁ *The secretary bird has long, skinny legs like a **wading bird**, and a body like an eagle.*

Sun bittern

Adult sun bitterns perform a special "broken wing" trick to protect their nest. If a predator approaches, the sun bittern will drag one wing along the ground as if it is broken. The predator will follow the apparently injured bird, thinking it will be easy to catch.

▷ *The "eyes" on a sun bitterns's wings make the bird's body look like the head of a much bigger, scarier animal.*

Fun fact!
*If any small fish, insects, or **crustaceans** touch the inside of a spoonbill's bill, the bird snaps it shut to catch them.*

Spoonbills

Spoonbills catch food by wading through shallow water swinging their open bill from side to side.

Sneaky animals

Some animals use sneaky methods to catch their prey or to escape from predators.

△ *The vampire bat quietly creeps along the ground up to its prey.*

Vampire bats

The common vampire bat is able to walk, jump, and hop. This means it can creep up to its prey and hop onto its body. As it bites, the bat's saliva enters the wound and makes the animal's skin go numb. The animal does not know it has been bitten.

Tarsiers

Tarsiers are related to monkeys and lemurs. They are found on islands in Southeast Asia. Tarsiers have good eyesight and hunt mostly at night. They pounce and grab the animal with their paws.

◁ *Tarsiers have large pads at the end of long fingers, to help grip branches and prey tightly.*

Raccoons

Raccoons are very sneaky. Their specially adapted paws can open latches and doors. They often steal food from houses, cars, and campsites.

△ *Raccoons often rifle through trash cans in search of food.*

Big mouth

Some birds, such as pelicans, have a huge mouth that they use to snap up large prey. Other birds use their mouth to alarm predators.

△ *If frightened, a tawny frogmouth opens its beak wide hoping to scare away predators.*

Tawny frogmouth

By day the tawny frogmouth sits very still in trees and is difficult to spot. At night, it hunts for insects, which it may dig from the soil or catch while flying.

Toucans

Toucans live in the rain forests of South America. They use their huge, colorful bills to pick fruit to eat. During the mating season, male and female toucans throw fruit at each other to attract a mate.

◁ *The toucan's large bill may discourage predators, but it is not strong enough to be used as a weapon.*

Pelicans

Pelicans are found on many of the world's coastlines. A large pouch hangs under their beak. They eat fish, frogs, and crustaceans, such as crabs and shrimps.

▷ *Pelicans expand their throat pouch to scoop prey out of the water.*

Fun fact!

In medieval times, it was thought that mother pelicans fed their young with their own blood when food was scarce.

Bizarre creatures

Reptiles and amphibians have some amazing habits. One lizard can actually run across water!

Common basilisk

A young common basilisk can run about 33 to 66 feet (10 to 20 meters) across the surface of water without sinking. It does this when fleeing from predators. The common basilisk eats insects, flowers, and small creatures, such as fish, snakes, and birds.

▷ *Webbing between the toes of the common basilisk helps it to run across water.*

▷ *Common rain frogs get their name from their habit of calling during rainstorms.*

Common rain frogs

Tiny common rain frogs live in rain forests and lay their eggs in a cup of leaves or on a moist patch of the forest floor. The eggs hatch into frogs rather than tadpoles.

Fun fact!

On land, the common basilisk rolls up its toe webbing.

Jackson's chameleon

The Jackson's chameleon comes from eastern Africa. The babies are born fully developed, rather than hatching from eggs.

▽ *The Jackson's chameleon is able to look in two directions at once. Males have three long horns.*

Beastly beetles

The ancient Egyptians believed that scarabs, or dung beetles, kept the world revolving like a huge ball of dung, or **feces**.

Dung beetles

Dung beetles live in many different **habitats**, including deserts, forests, and grasslands. They feed on the dung of plant-eating animals and squeeze and suck liquid out of the manure.

▽ *Using their back legs, some dung beetles roll animal dung into balls larger than themselves!.*

Burying beetles

Burying beetles bury dead creatures, such as birds or mice, in a hole in the soil. The female lays her eggs in the soil around the hole. When the eggs hatch, the larvae move into the dead body to feed.

△ Burying beetles use their antennae to detect dead animals from a long way off.

Stag beetles

Stag beetle larvae live for several years, eating rotting wood. The larvae change, or **metamorphose**, into beetles. In summer, the beetles fly about, rather clumsily, in search of mates.

▷ Male stag beetles use their enormous jaws to fight rival males for the best mating sites.

Pesky predators

Some reptiles and amphibians use a **lure** to attract prey. Others wait silently and then attack!

Alligator snapping turtle

The alligator snapping turtle has a small, wormlike growth on its tongue that it wriggles to attract prey, especially fish.

Death adders

Death adders bury themselves in sand or **leaf litter**, so that only the head and tail are visible. To attract prey, the death adder dangles the tip of its tail. When a bird or mammal tries to grab the "worm," the death adder poisons its prey in a fraction of a second.

◁ *The alligator snapping turtle's jaws are strong enough to bite off a human finger.*

◁ *The death adder has a thick body and a short tail.*

Surinam horned frog

The Surinam horned frog burrows itself into the ground and waits for prey. If a mouse, small lizard, or frog wanders past, the frog jumps out and grabs it.

Fun fact!

Some Surinam horned frog tadpoles will eat each other after they hatch.

▽ *The Surinam horned frog has patterned skin like a leaf which makes it difficult to see on the forest floor.*

Poisonous parts

Many fish and other water creatures use their poison in self-defense and not for attack.

Weevers

Weevers have poisonous spines on their gills and on their first dorsal fin (dorsal fins are on a fish's back). Weevers bury themselves in the seabed, leaving just their eyes poking out. As shrimps and small fish swim past, the weevers snap them up.

△ *The blue-ringed octopus is only the size of a golf ball, but it is one of the world's most poisonous animals.*

Blue-ringed octopuses

The blue-ringed octopus is a mollusk, not a fish. If attacked by a predator, it turns bright yellow with blue rings, and bites the attacker. Its poison is created by bacteria in the octopus's **salivary glands**. A single octopus carries enough poison to kill 26 adults.

◁ *The weever's poison is for defense. If a person stood on the fish, the fish's spines would sink into their foot.*

▽ *The stonefish is the most venomous fish in the world. It can be very difficult to spot among the reef's rocks.*

Stonefish

The stonefish lives on coral reefs. Its mottled colors provide good camouflage among the rocks. The dorsal fin on its back is covered in many venomous spines. The poison can be fatal to humans.

Fun fact!

Stonefish can spit out water, which is really unusual for a fish.

Terrifying tongues

Some animals have an amazing tongue—it may be forked, sticky, or just incredibly long.

△ An echidna hunts by poking its nose into the ground.

▽ *The okapi's tongue is 14 inches long (35 centimeters). It is as sensitive and flexible as a human hand.*

Echidnas

Echidnas, or spiny anteaters, have small nostrils and a tiny mouth at the end of their long, tubelike beaks. They eat ants and termites, which they catch with their long, sticky tongue.

Okapi

The okapi is brown with a stripy **rump** and legs. It is related to the giraffe and was only discovered in 1901. The okapi uses its long, black tongue to grab leaves and branches and pull them into its mouth.

Sun bear

The sun bear sleeps or sunbathes by day and hunts at night. It has long, curved claws, which it uses to dig for insects. It also pokes its long tongue into holes in rotten wood to catch insects or lick up honey.

▷ *The sun bear's slithery tongue is up to 10 inches long (25 centimeters).*

Fun fact!

If grabbed by the back of the neck, the sun bear can swivel its body around inside its loose neck skin to bite its attacker.

69

Creepy disguises

Many creepy crawlers use camouflage to hide from predators, while others use it so they can catch prey.

△ *The decorator crab* **camouflages** *itself all over so that predators find it hard to spot.*

▽ *The orchid mantis is a type of praying mantis. It has enlarged leg segments that resemble petals.*

Decorator crab

The decorator crab has small hooks on its back. It uses these to attach bits of seaweed, sponges, or sometimes sea anemones to itself. Predators are put off attacking, because sea anemones sting.

Flower mantids

Flower mantids are colored to look like the flowers on which they live. The mantids sit very still and wait for prey, such as flies, bees, butterflies, and moths, to come within reach. Then they pounce.

▽ *If threatened, the Macleay's specter stick insect sways like a dry leaf blowing in a breeze.*

The female Macleay's specter stick insect can curl her tail over her body like a scorpion.

Macleay's specter stick insect

A female stick insect can lay thousands of eggs in her lifetime. The eggs can take up to two years to hatch. The newly hatched young, called **nymphs**, resemble ants.

Stinky birds

Whether it is the birds themselves, their eggs, or the mess they make with their feces, some birds can be super stinky!

▷ *Giant petrels regurgitate foul-smelling oil into their gravel nests.*

Giant petrels

Northern and southern giant petrels lay stinky eggs. It is believed that the eggs smell to put off predators. The body of the southern giant petrel has a strong, musky smell, too.

Fun fact!

Starling feces is acidic and can damage buildings made of sandstone.

▷ The Hoopoe eats insects and worms. It has a colorful crest, which it raises when excited.

Hoopoes

The hoopoe makes a foul-smelling nest in a hole in a tree trunk or wall. It adds lots of feces to the nest to put off predators. It also squirts feces at intruders.

Starlings

Starlings are very common in the United Kingdom. The birds nest in spring, often in walls or attics. This can be a problem for homeowners, as the birds make lots of noise. Starling feces are not only smelly, but can also carry diseases.

◁ In winter, thousands of migrant starlings arrive in the United Kingdom from eastern Europe.

Tricky tongues

The tongues of some reptiles are extremely long and sticky. Some have tongues that are V-shaped, and some have brightly colored tongues.

Fun fact!
The sharp, venomous fangs of the diamondback rattlesnake can be more than 1 inch long (2.5 centimeters).

▽ *A Parson's chameleon can capture prey up to one-and-a-half body lengths away.*

Chameleons

When a chameleon sees prey, such as a grasshopper, it aims its long, sticky tongue at the animal. As the tip of the chameleon's tongue hits the prey, it forms a cup shape that sticks to the creature and traps it. The chameleon then pulls the insect into its mouth.

Diamondback rattlesnakes

The two species of diamondback rattlesnake are North America's most poisonous snakes. They warn predators of their presence by shaking the rattle at the end of their tail.

△ *The diamondback rattlesnake has a large, forked tongue.*

Blue-tongued skinks

Blue-tongued skinks sleep in leaf litter or fallen logs, and during the day hunt for snails, slugs, insects, spiders, berries, flowers, **fungi**, and **carrion**. Although their teeth are not sharp, they can give a powerful bite.

▷ *The blue-tongued skink sticks out its blue tongue to scare away predators.*

Slippery skins

Large slimy creatures can be found both on land and in the water. One of the most unusual is the axolotl. It has the unique ability to regrow parts of its body!

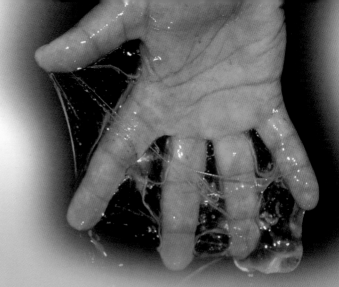

△ When slime eels are taken out of the water and handled, they drip with slime.

Worm lizards

There are more than 150 species of worm lizard. Their bodies are covered in scales amd they live underground. Most species do not have legs—they burrow by pushing the soil with their thick, bony skulls.

Slime eel

The slime eel is a deep-sea eel from the central north Pacific Ocean. It has a slitlike mouth and blunt head. The slime eel is a parasite. It burrows into the bodies of big fish.

▽ Unlike most worm lizards, the Mexican worm lizard, or ajolte, has strong front legs and sharp claws for digging.

▷ The axolotl has weak eyesight. To find food, it uses its sense of smell and special organs that help it to sense movement.

Axolotl

The axolotl lives in only a few freshwater canals near Mexico City. It is now an **endangered species**. If its habitat dries up, the axolotl loses its gills and it changes to become a land-living salamander.

Fun fact!

From the 1300s to the 1500s, the Aztec people of Mexico regularly ate axolotls as part of their diet.

77

Slimy fish

Fish produce slime from their skin. The slime protects them from parasites and diseases, and helps them to move through the water.

Hagfish

When threatened, hagfish ooze out a small amount of thick, white fluid. The fluid absorbs seawater and swells to form a thick, heavy slime. The slime suffocates predators by clogging their gills.

△ *At night, parrotfish secrete a mucus cocoon to mask their scent from predators.*

Parrotfish

The slimy cocoon that parrotfish sleep in at night provides good protection from parasites, which suffocate in the slime.

◁ *To get rid of its own slime, the hagfish ties itself in a knot and sweeps the knot toward its head to scrape itself clean.*

Slimeheads

Slimeheads are commonly known as roughies. They live in cold, deep waters. They breed later in life and live longer than most fish, up to 150 years!

▽ *Slimeheads, such as this southern roughy, have a network of slime-filled dents in their head.*

Ugly brutes

Some animals look ugly, they might have no hair, or have lumps on their faces, but these features are special adaptations that help the animals to survive.

△ *These naked mole rats are coming out of a tunnel in a zoo.*

Naked mole rat
The naked mole rat lives in long tunnels in the grassy regions of eastern Africa. Hairless skin means that the mole rat does not overheat in its underground home.

▽ *Adult male elephant seals have a large, fleshy nose used for making roaring noises during the mating season.*

Elephant seals
Elephant seals are huge creatures with folds of fat and skin. Their thick layer of fat is called blubber. It keeps them warm when they dive into the icy ocean to search for food.

A warthog's canine teeth grow constantly. It uses them to dig and search for food.

▽ *The four hard bumps on the warthog's face cushion the blows when it fights.*

Warthog

The male warthog has four hard bumps on its face that look like warts—from which it gets its name. Males and females have curved tusks, which they use as weapons, growing out of their mouths.

Gross eaters

Some animals have unpleasant eating habits. They may feast on dead animals or use their strong jaws to rip their prey apart.

△ *The wolverine's sharp, powerful claws help it to kill prey such as rabbits.*

Wolverine

The wolverine lives in Alaska, Siberia, northern Canada, and Scandinavia. It often eats the remains of animals killed by wolves but will also kill prey itself, by pouncing on an animal and tearing it apart.

Pangolins

Pangolins live in tropical Asia and Africa, and are covered with brown scales. The pangolin eats termites and ants which it sniffs out and catches on its long, sticky tongue. It has no teeth. Instead, horny plates in its stomach grind down the food.

▷ *The pangolin marks its territory by squirting a strong-smelling liquid from glands under its tail.*

▷ *The spotted hyena has large jaws which is uses to rip apart prey.*

Hyenas

Hyenas are strong, doglike creatures that live in Africa and India. Although they eat carrion, they also catch young hippos, gazelles, zebras, wildebeest, and antelopes. The stomach of a spotted hyena can hold a lot of meat, so it can go for several days without food.

Slimy bugs

Some slimy creatures cause problems for humans. Millipedes and froghoppers for example, can do severe damage to crops.

Maggots

"Maggot" is the name given to fly larvae. Some types of maggot, such as botfly larvae, are parasites. They live under the skin of living animals, causing sores, cuts, and even death.

▽ *The spotted snake millipede needs to stay damp and slimy.*

Fun fact!

Millipedes prefer to live in ground that has been covered in manure, or animal feces.

Snake millipedes

Snake millipedes live in leaf litter, under bark, and in moss. They are common in gardens throughout the UK. Snake millipedes use their 200 legs to climb trees.

◁ *Maggots hatch from flies'*
eggs. The flies lay their eggs on
rotten food and on the bodies
of dead animals.

Froghoppers

Froghoppers are small,
brown insects that can jump
27.5 inches (70 centimeters)
through the air to reach
the next plant. This is an
amazing distance for such
a tiny creature. Their larvae
are known as **nymphs**.
For protection, the nymphs
develop inside a blob of
froth, called cuckoo spit,
often seen on grass.

▷ *A froghopper nymph, or*
spittlebug, creates its protective
froth by blowing air into a fluid
excreted from its **anus**.

Scary beasts

Frightening myths and superstitions have been created around some animals so it's important to learn the truth...

Wolves

Wolves live in many northern countries. Gray wolves are fast runners, and chase down their prey. They hunt deer, elk, moose, hares, and beavers. Wolves live in organized packs of up to 20 animals.

◁ *Wolves have large, sharp teeth, which help to tear up meat.*

Aye-aye

The aye-aye lives in the rain forests of Madagascar. Using its long, bony middle finger, it taps on tree branches and listens for beetles and grubs moving under the bark. When it hears a grub moving, it picks it out of the bark using its long finger.

Fun fact!

Some people in Madagascar believe that a person will die if an aye-aye points its long middle finger at them.

▷ *The aye-aye's* **habitat** *is the tropical forest.*

Amazing adaptors

To help them to survive, some reptiles and amphibians have changed, or adapted, over time to new conditions.

Water storing frog

The water storing frog lives in Australia. The frog stores water in large quantities in its **bladder**. In hot conditions, it makes an underground hole, or cell. It may sleep there for several years, waiting for cooler, wetter weather.

Tokay

The tokay is a **gecko**. It has developed special clingy toe pads for gripping. The pads are covered in tiny hairs. The ends of these hairs are split into many parts. These tiny hairs can stick to smooth surfaces.

▷ *The tokay's soft, velvety skin is colored to help it blend in with tree bark.*

◁ *The water storing frog is only seen after heavy rain.*

Sirens

Sirens live in the southern United States, in shallow pools and ditches. When their pools dry up, sirens burrow into the mud and make a **cocoon** out of hardened slime and old skin. They can survive in their cocoon for up to two years.

▷ Sirens have a horny, beaklike mouth and a pair of tiny front legs, but no back legs.

89

Glossary

Adapted
Animals that have changed over many generations to suit their living conditions.

Algae
Certain types of plants that grow in or near water. Algae do not have ordinary leaves or roots.

Amazon basin
The Amazon basin is the part of South America drained by the Amazon River.

Amphibians
Animals that can live both on land and in water, such as frogs, toads, newts, and salamanders.

Anacondas
Anacondas are large snakes that kill prey animals by crushing them with their body.

Antarctica
Antarctica is the huge, cold continent around the South Pole. It is twice the size of Australia.

Antennae
Long feelers on the heads of insects and crustaceans.

Anus
The hole in the body from which feces are pushed out.

Appendage
A body part, such as an arm, leg, tail, or fin.

Aquarium
A glass container in which fish and other water creatures and plants are kept. It can also be a type of zoo that you can visit to see many different types of fish and other water creatures in tanks and pools.

Bacteria
Very small organisms that are found everywhere. Some bacteria cause illnesses, such as stomach upsets.

Biologists
Scientists who study the science of living things, such as plants and animals.

Bladder
The bladder is an organ found in the bodies of humans and animals. It stores urine, which is produced by the kidneys.

Bony fish
A bony fish has a skeleton made of bone. Most fish are bony fish, but some fish, such as sharks, have skeletons made completely of stretchy cartilage.

Calcium
Bones, teeth, and shells are made of calcium, which is a natural material. Calcium is essential for the normal growth and development of most animals and plants.

Camouflage
An animal that is camouflaged is difficult to spot because its patterns or colours blend in with the background.

Carrion
The dead or decaying flesh of an animal.

Cocoon
A cocoon is a silky pouch spun by the larvae of many insects, such as silkworms and caterpillars. It covers the larva and keeps it safe as it develops into an adult.

Crayfish
A lobster-like, freshwater creature.

Crustacean
A type of animal that has a hard outer shell. They live in water, such as crabs, shrimps, or lobsters, or on land, such as wood lice.

Cub
The name given to the young of some animals, such as bears, lions, and tigers.

Dabbling duck
Shallow-water ducks, including shovelers, that feed by bobbing forward and under the water so as to feed off the bottom.

Dinosaurs
Dinosaurs were reptiles that became extinct a very long time ago. One of the best known was Tyrannosaurus rex.

Endangered
An endangered species is in danger of dying out or becoming extinct.

Extinct
If a species is extinct, it has died out—none of its kind are living.

Extinction
When the last of a species dies, that species is said to be extinct. No more individuals exist.

Eyestalks
Movable stalks with an eye at their tip. They are found in crustaceans, such as crabs, and in some molluscs, such as snails.

Fangs
Long, sharp teeth. In a snake, fangs are often hollow and are used to inject venom into their prey.

Feces
Waste matter that passes out from an animal's anus.

Ferment
To make a substance change chemically from one state to another. When vegetation ferments inside a bird, it is broken down by living substances, such as yeast or bacteria, into a different state.

Fungi
Plants without leaves or flowers, such as mushrooms and toadstools. They grow on other plants or decayed material.

Gecko
Geckos are small reptiles. They have toe pads that can stick to smooth surfaces. Some people keep geckos as pets.

Gill rakers
Bony, finger-like sticks found in the gills of some fish. The gill rakers help to support the gills.

Gills
Gills are the organs that help animals that live in water to breathe. The gills take oxygen from the water.

Gulf of California
Part of the Pacific Ocean between the coast of Mexico and the peninsula of Lower California.

Habitat
The natural surroundings of an animal.

Immune
To be protected from, or not affected by, something, such as a disease or poison.

Inflate
To inflate is to get larger, usually by filling with gas. A balloon inflates when you blow into it.

Larva
The newly hatched stage of certain creatures, such as butterflies and ladybugs. Larvae change to become quite different-looking creatures as adults.

Leaf litter
Dead plant material made from decaying leaves, twigs, and bark.

Lichen
A type of dry-looking fungus with many tiny branches. Lichen grows on rocks and trees.

Lure
A lure is something such as an antenna, or strange-shaped tail, which looks like an insect or a worm. It is used by predators to attract creatures that will want to eat the lure, so that they instead may be caught.

Mammal
Mammals are warm-blooded animals with backbones and hair. They produce live young, not eggs. There are around 5400 species of mammals, ranging from the huge blue whale to the tiny bumblebee bat.

Maneater
A large creature that kills a person in an unprovoked attack is described as a maneater. Sharks and tigers, for example, can become maneaters.

Metamorphose
When an animal goes through metamorphosis, it changes completely. A caterpillar changes into a butterfly or moth, and a tadpole changes into a frog.

Nectar
Nectar is a sugary liquid produced by plants. Some birds, such as hummingbirds, drink nectar. As they do so, they pollinate the plants that make the nectar, and this enables the plants to produce new seeds.

Nocturnal
Animals that are nocturnal are active at night, when they move around and hunt for food. During the day, they rest and sleep.

Northern hemisphere
The half of the Earth between the North Pole and the equator.

Nymph
The young or larval stage of some animals. Nymphs change into a different form as they become adults.

Predator
A creature that hunts and kills other animals for food.

Prehistoric
Belonging to very ancient times. Dinosaurs were alive in prehistoric times—the time before recorded history.

Prey
An animal that is hunted and killed for food by another animal.

Radula
A radula is a mollusc's flexible tongue. It has horny teeth, used for scraping up food.

Rain forest
Dense tropical forests found in areas of very heavy rainfall.

Regurgitate
To bring food back into the mouth after it has been swallowed.

Reptile
Cold-blooded animals that have a backbone and short legs or no legs at all, such as snakes, lizards, and crocodiles.

Rice paddies
Flooded fields used for growing rice.

Rodents
A group of animals that includes mice, voles, squirrels, and shrews.

Rump
The backside or buttocks of a large animal.

Saliva
The liquid produced in the mouth to keep it moist and to help break down and swallow food.

Salivary glands
Salivary glands are found in the mouth. They make saliva, which is the liquid that we call spit or spittle.

Scavenger
A scavenger hunts for and eats dead animals, or carrion. Vultures and hyenas are scavengers. They feed on the bodies of animals that have been killed by predators.

Secrete
To secrete means to release liquid, especially from glands in the body.

Snout
The projecting nose and mouth of an animal.

Species
A group of animals that share characteristics. Animals of the same species can breed with each other.

Spur
A sharp, bony spike on the back of an animal's leg.

Suction
The act of sucking. Some animals have suction cups on their feet or legs that help them to grip their prey or slippery, steep surfaces.

Tadpoles
The newly hatched young of creatures such as frogs, toads, and newts.

Tapirs
A tapir is a creature with a heavy body and short legs, similar in shape to a pig. It is related to the horse and the rhinoceros.

"Third eye"
An organ that detects, or senses, light, found on the head of some reptiles.

Toxin
A poisonous substance, especially one formed in the body.

T-rex
T-rex is short for Tyrannosaurus rex—probably the most famous of the large, meat-eating dinosaurs.

Tropical
Tropical relates to the tropics—the area on either side of the equator. The tropics are usually hot and damp.

Tussocks
Clumps or tufts of growing grass.

Venom
The poison used by some mammals, snakes and spiders to paralyze or kill their prey.

Wading bird
A wading bird is a long-legged shore bird, such as a sandpiper or curlew.

Wetlands
Wetlands are naturally wet areas, such as marshes or swamps. They have spongy soil.

Index

Picture Credits